"Thank you for the beautiful tap melody",

a student tells me after class,

and I remember why I love to teach tap.

Teaching
the Beauty of a Tap Melody

Bibliografische Information der Deutschen Nationalbibliothek:
Die Deutsche Nationalbibliothek verzeichnet diese Publikation in der
Deutschen Nationalbibliografie; detaillierte bibliografische Daten sind im
Internet über http://dnb.dnb.de abrufbar.

Illustrations: Birgit Brade

Herstellung und Verlag: BoD – Books on Demand, Norderstedt

ISBN: 978-3-754-3184-78

CONTENTS

Teaching
the Beauty of a Tap Melody

PRACTICAL INSTRUCTIONS AND IMPULSES

FOR TEACHING TAP DANCE

Birgit Brade

 # Preparation

It is shortly before class.

On a good day I have a perfectly planned preparation for class with a fine warm-up and exercises for technique and rhythm. The exercises elegantly lead to new material and at the end of the well-timed lesson we still have time to repeat the material from last week.

On a different day I rush into class, stressed and unprepared. I spontaneously think of a warm-up and the whole lesson will be improvised.

Both of it may work out really well or not so well.

The difference is that I am much better with preparation in the background - I am relaxed, I can also deviate from the structure if, as almost always happens, something goes differently than I had imagined and I am open and attentive to my students.

I have been a tap dancer and teacher for over 25 years, and especially at the beginning of this time I often wished for a book that would have helped me with practical guidance for teaching tap. There are books that have inspired me personally as a tap dancer, most notably Acia Gray's *The Souls of your Feet*, Brenda Bufalino's *Tapping the Source* and Rusty Frank's *Tap*! Unfortunately, there were none that would have been specifically helpful for my classes, so over the course of many hours of practice, preparation and teaching, I developed my own concept, which I suspect will remain in constant evolution.

When I started teaching, I knew exactly three short choreographies and had had regular tap dance lessons myself for two years. (Many thanks at this point to Irina Maué, who awakened my enthusiasm and laid the foundations for this very special dance form that combines dance and music).

Before I taught a tap dance class for the first time, I didn't know much about music and rhythm - most of it had worked intuitively until then. But now it was necessary to understand what I was doing so that I could explain how choreographies are structured, how music is constructed and how music and steps relate to each other.

I had also only thought about technique as much as I needed to be able to reproduce what I had learned in class as well as possible.

However, coming up with choreographies or exercises myself seemed to be the biggest challenge. I accepted the challenge and started to think about everything that lies behind the steps, combinations, choreographies and exercises.

And I thought about teaching, that is, about how I could bring the participants closer to everything that tap dance is for me.

In this book I try to describe these reflections and my teaching concept, hoping that it can be helpful to other tap dance teachers.

Of course, my concept is not finished - with every lesson, every new group and every new participant, something new happens that helps me to develop. This is therefore my personal interim report for you!

The first chapters correspond to the possible contents of a lesson or workshop. I don't teach every section in every class, but I always start with a warm-up, and there is almost always one or more exercises on technique and/or rhythm. Since we usually work on a choreography, there is almost always a new step combination and repetitions of the material already learned.

I offer improvisation exercises from time to time; in some groups more often, in other groups less often.

Body percussion is a whole area of its own - some exercises are suitable here as a warm-up; but I also teach a complete body percussion choreography from time to time.

At the end of the book I have added a few reflections on music.

Each chapter contains concrete exercises and reflections on the respective topic. The exercises are designed for groups, but can also be done in groups of two or in individual lessons without any problems.

In principle, all exercises practice rhythm and technique (and posture and balance), and most of the exercises can also be used as warm-up exercises.

Some of the exercises I have learnt over the years in workshops, seminars and further training with other teachers in the fields of tap dance, movement and dance improvisation and sometimes modified and/or extended, others I have invented myself. At the end of the book you will find a list of tap dancers, dancers and teachers who have supported me in my development.

REFLECTIONS ON GROUP CONSTELLATIONS

CHILDREN'S GROUPS:

For me, the biggest challenge in tap dance classes are groups of children. I recommend tap for children from the age of seven or eight at the earliest because, whichever way you look at it, tap dance is definitely quite technical and demanding in every way.
Children love tap dance, but realise very quickly that it is not as easy as other types of dance, but rather comparable to learning an instrument. The ease and rhythmic precision that is so inspiring in tap dance can only be achieved through a lot of practice.
 Nevertheless, I design the lessons in the children's groups less technically than with the adults. Most of the time, the warm-up is also a (tap) game and sometimes we play games that focus on rhythm, improvisation or attention.
With younger children, teaching new content is not so much explaining as showing - imitation is often the most reliable way for primary school children to learn.

There are no homogeneous groups, and with children it is really a big challenge to reconcile the differences. Often, some are already bored while others have not yet grasped a certain technique or combination.   In this case, it sometimes makes sense to differentiate. This means that those who can and want to do more get the current combination in an extended version. It is also possible that some dance the current combination in quarters and others twice as fast, i.e. in eighth notes. One problem that can arise when differentiating is the pressure of competition that exists to a greater or lesser extent, depending on the respective groups.

The weaker participants do not necessarily want to be seen as weaker; besides, they also want to learn the "cool", more difficult combination. And that's what they should do. You have to decide in the current situation what the best method is.

Sometimes I form groups of two and let the children explain the new step to each other and practise together. My task then is more to monitor and help.

The nice thing about children's groups is that the participants are very energetic and motivated when they dance. Up to the age of about eleven or twelve, most of them also have a lot of fun performing or improvising. (For exercises see chapter "Creativity" and "Improvisation")

MIXED ADULT GROUPS

Whether children's, youth or adult groups - different personalities with different previous knowledge and talents, different preferences in terms of music and dance style and their own ideas of teaching always come together here.

Heterogeneity is also an issue with adults; however, in my experience, adults are often more patient and welcome long practice sequences and repetitions rather than finding them tiring. Nevertheless, it can be useful to differentiate here as well. Most adults have fewer problems with differentiating/classifying into weaker and stronger groups, so that it is possible to work with exciting complementary rhythmic figures.

TEENAGE GROUPS

I really like to work with youths because on the one hand they are mostly open for exciting rhythmical experiments, on the other hand they don't shy away from intensely working on technique and precision. Quite the opposite!
Besides, most young students easily memorize choreographies and in general the learning pace is high, which keeps the lessons exciting. What is more, children and youths often contribute to the lessons with their own ideas and suggestions for exercises and choreographies.

50PLUS-GROUPS

Participants who start tap-dancing when they are 50 years or older are always highly motivated and attentive, but most of them also approach the matter with composure. These groups, like others are always heterogeneous, but older students usually are more tolerant, so that extensive practise and repetition is welcomed.

What always pleases me is, that with these groups the motivation is relatively high to present what they have learned.
Planning a joint performance always sets free energies - all of a sudden the students organize themselves independently from the lessons to practice together!

MY PERSONAL NOTATION FOR TAP DANCE COMBINATIONS

Fortunately, today it is possible to film combinations and choreographies easily with your smartphone in order to archive them or to practise.

However, I still write down combinations by hand. In that way I am forced to reflect the matter on a theoretical level and, furthermore, the steps retain in my memory more easily.

There are several possibilities to notate tap dance combinations; here I would like to briefly introduce my method.

First of all I create three columns; in the left one I write down the rhythm; in the middle there are the steps, and in the right column you see which foot has to be used and if necessary further instructions like: do we travel in a specific direction; do we turn... The quarter notes are always written as whole numbers, that is **1,2,3**... With a binary rhythm the **+** defines the eighth notes and the **e** the sixteenth notes. With a ternary rhythm the **+** and the **e** define the triplets. The **de** in a binary rhythm stands for an eighth triplet or in a binary rhythm for a thirty-second note . A rest is written **(...)**. As is usual in dance, I combine two bars together, that is, in a four-four time, I count to eight.

With a binary rhythm, it could look like this:

1	shuf-	r
+2	fle step	r r
3	shuf-	l
+4	fle step	l l
5	shuf-	r
+6	fle step	r r
e+e7	heel heel ball ball	r l r l
8	clap	

A combination in a ternary rhythm could look like this:

e1	heel dig	l r
+e2	brush (b) step heel	r r r
e3	heel shuf-	r l
+e4	fle step heel	l l l
e5	heel dig	l r
+e6	brush (b) step heel	r r r
7	stamp	l
(8)	----	

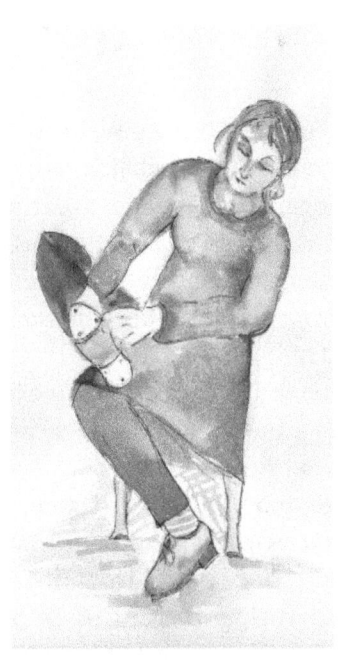

 # Warm-Up

THE PURPOSE OF A WARM-UP EXERCISE

I start every lesson with a warm-up exercise.

This part is intended to create a good initial feeling and a relaxed basis for learning. Furthermore we want to warm up our muscles to avoid injuries and increase our mobility.

According to my concept that means: a warm-up exercise should not be a challenge but it should make the participants feel safe while they can relate to their skills and knowledge.

With absolute beginners an appropriate exercise could be Part 1 of Warm-Up Exercise 1.

But you can keep in mind: a concept of an exercise or of a lesson has to be understood as a frame; its contents can be varied according to interaction, group or atmosphere.

If I realize, that the students are struggling, I simplify the exercise. According to the first warm-up-exercise, that could mean to extend the phases and/or introduce easier rhythm patterns.

If I notice that the participants want to be challenged, I accordingly offer a higher tempo and/or more complicated rhythm patterns.

WARM-UP EXERCISE 1

CRISSCROSS

We walk crisscross through the room; I take the lead, the students follow to the beat of a simple music. Simple means: the music should range in a four-four time in a medium tempo which for me lies between 90 to 110 bpm. For you it can sure be different.

Part 1:

To start off, we walk with *flats* on the fourth notes until everyone moves easily to the beat.

Next, the walking pace changes, that is, for a while I walk in half tempo - again, until everyone gets used to this change and then I change to eighth notes, that is double time.

With a higher tempo you should move from *flats* to *steps.*

Part 2:

I introduce a simple rhythm pattern that spans a bar and is repeated in a loop. At first we use only *steps* and *flats*; during the exercise we can extend our repertoire. As we did in Part 1 the rhythm continues for a while until I introduce a new one.

Part 3:

The students take turns leading.

WARM-UP EXERCISE 2

ECHO

I stand at the front with my back to the group (standard line-up for demonstration); the group is standing in rows, so that every dancer can see me. Again, I choose a piece of music that ranges in medium tempo. Whether I use a binary or ternary rhythm depends on the material that I want to teach later in the lesson. If I want to teach a combination in swing, it might be preferable to choose a warm-up-exercise with that rhythm. Then I dance a combination spanning one bar that is repeated by the students in the following bar. Afterwards I tap-dance a different combination that is also repeated and so on.

You should start with easy rhythmical combinations, consisting for example of **steps** only, after a while you might combine **steps** with **step-heels** and/or **shuffles**.

I don't do a fixed set of combinations here; I improvise the respective bars and I often repeat on the left side what I did on the right side . During the exercise I increase the level of difficulty - but I never proceed in the same way - it depends on the respective group, their level and structure and ultimately on the mood of the day.

WARM-UP EXERCISES – (NOT EXCLUSIVELY) FOR CHILDREN

In the following I will introduce several warm-up-exercises that are particularly suitable for children. However they might also go down well with adult groups.

WARM-UP EXERCISE 3

SNAKE

We stand in line, like a snake. The first dancer - the head of the snake - takes a lead. That means, the snake moves crisscross through the room, imitating the leader's moves. The music should be dynamic with a clear rhythmical structure. If we do the exercise for the first time, I usually start as the head.

We don't want to perform complicated tap combinations, the leader should much rather react to the music and for example walk with *steps* and *flats* in a specific rhythmical pattern. It is also possible to move sideways or backwards, or to perform turns or stops. It is important to carry out the movement repeatedly for a while so that everyone can join in. After a while the leader waves good-bye, runs to the end of the snake and the next participant performs as the leader.

You will notice, that children as well as adults will become rather creative; you can extend or change the rules together.

WARM-UP EXERCISE 4

DOPPELGANGER

The participants form groups of two. If there's an odd number of dancers, I also take a partner.

Initially, every group chooses a space and agrees on who will lead. Then the exercise works similar to SNAKE.

One dancer leads, the other follows; similar to the snake exercise a particular movement or combination is performed repeatedly for a while. Both partners move synchronously before the next movement is introduced.

I suggest, that we dance on the spot as well as using the whole space, just as we like. The participants may move one in front of the other or in a row.

After some time I suggest switching roles; the students might as well decide on their own when it is time to switch.

Variation 1:

The leader taps first, the follower second, like in ECHO.

Variation 2:

If I or somebody else calls "switch" the groups have to re-form which always makes for a stimulating dynamic.

 # Rhythm

Rhythm is the heart of tap dance and the brain and the nervous system. Rhythm can be grasped and expressed intuitively; additionally we are able to understand and practice rhythmical patterns cognitively.

While tap dancing, we make rhythm audible; drumming with our feet, playing music with our body.

It happens frequently that somebody tells me: "I would really like to learn tap dancing, but I'm totally lacking any feeling for rhythm." Actually, in my opinion, everybody has a feeling for rhythm even if it is hidden somewhere; so that with some people it takes some time to get back to this sense. There are certain methods, exercises and strategies, to strengthen the sense for rhythm; some of those I want to introduce in this chapter.

BASIC CONCEPTS OF RHYTHM

Before we can talk about rhythm, I want to provide you with several basic definitions of rhythmical terms, the way I use them. If you prefer different definitions - no problem; there are always various possibilities. Here are my suggestions:

Rhythm:

A certain amount of beats/notes in a set time; the notes appear in a certain order with a particular length and are emphasized or not.

Bar:

Section of time, that organizes notes and gives a structure for pieces of music and/or choreographies. In European music you most often find quadruple metres. 5/4, 6/8, 7/8 bars are possible, but rare. They can occasionally be found in jazz music.

Note values:

Fourth note - the pulse/beat underlying the rhythm;

a four-quarter time has four fourth notes;

those correspond to one whole note, two half notes, eight eighth notes etc.

In tap dance, the notes surely have no real duration, here the note values refer to the intervals between the notes.

Triplets:

Quarter triplet - three equal beats per fourth note

Eighth triplet - three equal beats per eighth note

Sixteenth triplet - three equal beats per sixteenth note

Binary rhythm:

An even rhythm on the basis of eighth notes, fourth notes etc.

Ternary rhythm:

A rhythm on the basis of triplets

Time Step:

Traditionally, a time step is a simple combination at the beginning of a routine that enables the dancers to synchronise with each other and the musicians.

RHYTHM EXERCISE 1

SYNCHRONISATION & ATTENTION EXERCISE

We stand in a circle. I set a tempo by counting the fourth notes: "Five, six, seven, eight!" Then I start on count one with a *clap* and we continue clapping evenly one after the other. This sounds easier than it is. I suggest that everyone bounces on every beat, so that the pulse remains in the body even if it is not your turn.

When there is a evenness after a few rounds, I introduce a new element.

Variation 1:

With a *double-clap*, the direction is changed. Each participant may double-clap for a change of direction.

Variation 2:

We are doing the exercise with our eyes closed

Variation 3:

Breaks are introduced: if a participant steps back, there is a break in this position. The more people perform a break, the greater the challenge and also the fun. Usually I do this part without changing directions and with open eyes, but you sure can experiment by changing or extending the rules.

RHYTHM EXERCISE 2

TELEPHONE GAME

I call this exercise "Telephone Game" because it reminds me of this children's game.

We stand in a circle and I set a time by counting to four . Then I introduce a rhythm that goes over a four-four time. This rhythm is now supposed to go through the circle. That means, every participant claps the rhythm he or she remembers; one after the other. It makes sense to start with easy rhythms and after a few rounds you can increase the level of difficulty.

This exercise also helps to develop a feeling for musical structures and to survey the duration of a bar. The students also learn to start on count one. You can help them by emphasizing the one in every bar.

Variation 1

We walk with *flats* on the half notes (on 1,3 etc.) while performing the above explained exercise.

Variation 2

The participants themselves introduce the rhythm - one after the other. Everything else stays the same.

Variation 3

Now the rhythm that is introduced, has to be tap-danced. Here again you should start with easy combinations and by and by increase the level.

RHYTHM EXERCISE 3

FOURTH, EIGHTH AND HALF NOTES

We stand in a circle. I start with **heel drops** (=**heels**) evenly in a medium tempo - the heels are on the fourth notes. When everyone has joined in, I add the eighth notes by clapping them. After a while I also add the half notes - by clicking my tongue (or calling out "Ha" or whatever comes to your mind).

Variation 1

We are doing heels as fourth notes over two bars, then claps as eighth notes over two bars; then the half notes tongue clicking, also over two bars.
Afterwards I divide the group into three smaller groups and we perform a round: the first group starts: two bars of fourth, two bars of eighth and two bars of half notes. After the first two bars, the second group joins in, then the third, so that the three groups create a canon.

Extension

The students form groups of two and make up small combinations for every part. Breaks should be included!

Then every group shows their results.

Finally, all groups can dance their combinations together at the same time.

It is also possible to let the dancers try out their pieces with music.

RHYTHM EXERCISE 4

ORCHESTRA

I divide the group into two groups facing each other. Then I present a small tap dance combination to the first group. They are supposed to perform the combination in a loop. When the loop is going well, I turn to the second group and give a different combination to them. Both combinations should be performed simultaneously, overlapping each other for a while until I turn to the first group to provide them with a new combination and so forth.

Variation 1

Instead of two groups there are three or more groups; apart from that, everything proceeds as described.

Variation 2

One of the participants takes my position as the leader/conductor of the "orchestra".

 # Technique

GENERAL CONSIDERATIONS CONCERNING TECHNIQUE IN TAP DANCE

One of the principal pillars in tap dance is the technique.

My understanding of technique refers to the way we produce sound in tap-dancing. Contrary to common assumptions, the whole body is involved here.

Therefore, in my opinion, body posture as a basis for movement also belongs to technique.

In order to perform a movement in tap-dancing, it is important, that the dancer has at the same time an appropriate looseness as well as enough body tension. Legs and feet should mostly be relaxed; and a particular tension in your abdomen helps to protect your back and stabilize the movement.

It helps to adopt a flexible posture with slightly bent knees. Sometimes, though, we work with more or less bent or stretched legs, which depends on the quality of the movement. While tap dancing we stay a lot on the balls of our feet, so that for helping to keep our balance, we should transfer the weight (the upper body) slightly to the front without rounding the back.

In tap dance the footwork is essential, but I have to point out that every foot movement is initiated from the core.

To produce a sound with your foot, you use your whole leg moving from the hip.

You should try to do shuffles from the ankle and afterwards with your whole leg. You will clearly feel the difference: in the first case, the movement will be more strenuous, whereas the shuffles with your whole leg are more relaxed and powerful.

In the following I want to give you a list of tap techniques with short definitions. Some terms might vary from teacher to teacher or from region to region.

Look at it as my personal tap dance language!

TERMS AND DEFINITIONS

(This list is not complete, and it might differ in detail from what you learned and teach yourself. Feel free, to add terms or translate them into your own tap language.)

ONE SOUND STEPS

step
you step onto the ball of your foot, shifting your weight and producing a sound

flat
the whole foot - heel and ball - touches the floor

stamp
a flat with weight shift

stomp
a flat without weight shift

brush (back/forward)
the ball of your foot strikes the floor while moving the leg forward or back

tap
the ball of your foot touches the floor - the movement is performed from top down and then the foot is lifted again

heel (drop)
the heel strikes the floor with or without a weight shift

(heel) dig
the edge of the heel hits the floor

scuff
while the leg swings forward, the trailing edge of the heel strikes the floor

toe
the tip of the shoe hits the floor

ball (drop)
the ball "drops" to the floor

hop
a jump that is initiated from the weight bearing foot - and you land on the same side

leap
you jump from one side to the other, landing on the ball of your foot

jump
starting with your weight on both feet, you jump and again land on both feet

chug
the foot slides forward on the ball of your feet - into the heel; can be done with one foot or both

heel click
lift your heels and click them together

toe click
lift the balls of your feet and click them together

heel-to-toe-click
while swinging forward, one heel touches the ball of the weight-bearing leg

toe-to-heel-click
swing your leg backwards and touch the *heel* of your weight-bearing leg with the other *ball*

slide
while dragging your foot over the floor, you make a scraping noise

clap
clap your hands

TWO SOUND STEPS

ball change
two consecutive *steps*, the first one moves to the front, the second to the back (or the other way round)

shuffle
do a *brush* forward, followed by a *brush* back. Move with the relaxed, lifted leg top down and slightly forward and backward. With the second *brush*, the leg moves back up.

scuffle
like a *shuffle* , but replace the *brush* by a *scuff*

step heel
combine step and *heel*, usually with a weight shift

flap
combine a short *brush* forward with a *step*. A *flap* is usually done syncopated. It's a top down movement!

flam
the foot is put down from above - first the *ball*, followed by the **heel**

slap
like *flap*, but without shifting the weight

riff

while swinging to the front, the front edge of the ball touches the floor; the ball is pulled upwards and the back edge of the heel touches the floor

pull back

jumping upwards the ball touches the floor; you land on the same side or on the other (**pull back change**)

THREE SOUND STEPS

snap (also slurp or third)

works similarly to the **slap**, but the foot is dragged relatively flat across the floor; three sounds result from this movement: the first one at the front edge of the ball, the second one at the back edge of the heel and the third while stretching the leg, doing a **ball drop**

riffle

the movement is similar to doing a **snap**, but the third sound is done upwards, lifting the foot

wing

jumping upwards the balls slide outwards, and still in the air both balls touch the floor with am inward movement followed by landing on the balls of the foot

FOUR SOUND STEPS

cramp roll (basic)
we slightly jump up and land on ***step step heel heel - r, l, r, l or l, r, l, r***
The four beats of the ***cramp roll*** are done evenly and quickly - for example on **+e de 1**

round cramp roll
we proceed like above, though the ***step step heel heel*** is **done r, l, l, r or l, r, r, l**

pressed cramp roll
 = ***heel flam heel***

shuffle roll
 = ***shuffle step heel***

HERE IS SPACE FOR YOUR ADDITIONS:

TECHNIQUE EXERCISES

There are countless possibilities to practise technique. For example, if you introduce a new technique, it can be useful to let the students try out this new element for some time. To practise methodically, it has proven to be useful, to use a structure that has two bars (eight counts) as a basis. That is, if *shuffles* are introduced, you do seven *shuffles* on one side plus one weight transfer (step or flat), then you reverse etc.. Of course, it's most fun with music!

Apart from this easy method, I want to provide you with several specific technique exercises.

TECHNIQUE EXERCISE 1

SHUFFLES IN DIFFERENT POSITIONS

I stand in front of the group, the participants stand in rows behind me.

You can do this exercise with or without music; choose a tempo that suits you.

I start with **shuffles** on the right next to the left foot. Again, I point out that **shuffles** should be initiated from the hip with your whole relaxed leg. It's a top down movement. Let your **shuffle** become very small, if you want to become fast and precise.

The structure of the exercise looks like this:

e1	shuffle	r
e2	shuffle	r
e3	shuffle	r
e4	shuffle	r
e5	shuffle	r
e6	shuffle	r
e7	shuffle	r
8	flat	r

This part is reversed, then you do it again on both sides to complete **Part A**.

Part B:

For Part B, the structure stays the same, but you do your *shuffles* at the side. For this purpose, I bend the weight-bearing leg (l) and take the stretched leg (r) to the side, so that the left side of the ball of the foot touches the floor doing the *shuffles*.

Part C:

The same as **A** and **B**, but I bend the weight-bearing leg even more and the *shuffle* is done diagonally backwards.

Part D:

Here I cross the *shuffle* over the weight-bearing foot, so that the first *brush* goes forward and the second over the foot; for the second *shuffle*, the movement is reversed. The structure of the exercise again stays the same.

There might be even more possibilities to extend or vary this exercise - let your creativity flow!

Of course, you can shorten the exercise, if you realize, that a group is actually not motivated to do long, steady exercises. But every so often such meditative, steady practise goes down well. Usually I try to keep an eye on the atmosphere and react spontaneously to it.

TECHNIQUE EXERCISE 2

THIS AND THAT (BASICS)

This exercise is suitable as a technique-exercise and as a warm-up-exercise.

If you do it as a warm-up-exercise, you should use slow music; if the participants are already warmed up, a higher tempo can be useful.

Mostly, I perform this exercise with music; I start with easy steps, for example with *step-heels.* The students join in. Usually after eight bars, I change to a variation, for instance *shuffle step-heel*, after another eight bars (or less or more) I change the combination again. If I perform longer combinations, it makes sense to do it over a longer period. The exercise could be structured like this:

8 bars: *step heel*

8 bars: *shuffle step heel*

8 bars: *dig brush step heel*

16 bars: *dig brush heel shuffle step heel*

etc.

TECHNIQUE EXERCISE 3

SHUFFLE-HEEL EXERCISE

This exercise is done in triplets - here, we again practice *shuffles* in different positions - now combined with *heels*.

We start on the right side with our weight on the left foot; the position of the *shuffles* is at the front beside the left foot. We always do two *shuffles* plus one *heel*; at the end of the sequence we replace the *heel* by a *flat* to change sides.

e1	shuffle	r
+e2	shuffle heel	r l
e3	shuffle	r
+e4	shuffle heel	r l
e5	shuffle	r
+e6	shuffle heel	r l
e7	shuffle	r
+e8	shuffle flat	r r

Then we do the exercise on the left side (with our weight on the right side) and repeat both sides again. That is **Part A.**

Part B:

The structure stays the same, but the *shuffles* are now done to the side. We bend our knee of our leg-bearing leg a bit more.

Part C:

The structure stays the same, but the *shuffles* are now done diagonally backwards. The knee of our leg-bearing leg is bent even more, the foot doing the shuffle touches the floor with the inner edge of the ball.

Part D:

Again, the structure is the same, but the first *shuffle* is executed at the front, the second to the side.

Part E:

The structure is the same, but the first *shuffle* is executed to the side, the second to the back.

Part F:

While using the same structure, the first *shuffle* crosses over the weight-bearing foot, the second moves back.

TECHNIQUE EXERCISE 4

RIFFLES AND SNAPS (=THIRDS)

We stand in a circle and move clockwise . The structure of the exercise is as follows:

e de 1	riffle	r
e de 2	snap	r
e de 3	riffle	l
e de 4	snap	l
e de 5	riffle	r
e de 6	snap	r
e de 7	snap	l
e de 8	snap	r

We reverse and repeat the exercise several times.

Variation 1

Add a *heel* after every *riffle* and every *snap*!

Variation 2

Add a *heel* before **and** after every *riffle* and every *snap*!

54

 # Improvisation

From my perspective, the aim of all efforts in tap dance is to be able to use your repertoire for improvisation. The aim of most of my students is to avoid improvisation as far as possible. For me, improvisation means the greatest possible freedom in expressing myself in tap. For many students, improvisation means the greatest possible uncertainty.

Over the years I realized, that my personal aims are not necessarily the same for my students. Many participants are happy with learning choreographies and developing their skills in technique, rhythm and precision without deepening the subject of improvisation.

Nevertheless, I still sometimes teach improvisation, but the most important thing for me is, that my students feel good and have fun. Therefore, I try to create improvisation exercises, that let the participants feel safe, by providing them with a structure and/or well-known elements.

But there are of course always groups or students, that really like improvisation. That's why I want to share some improvisation exercises with you.

The warm-up-exercises that include parts, where the participants themselves take a lead, can also be seen as improvisation exercises.

IMPROVISATION EXERCISE 1

OVERLAY WITH STEPS & SHUFFLES

Part A

We stand in a circle and start together with a simple combination including *steps* and *shuffles*. It might look like this:

1	step	r
2	step	l
3	shuf-	r
+4	fle step	r r

=> Reverse and repeat several times!

Part B

Afterwards I give an example for extending the combination by doing double *shuffles* or adding *steps* or even leaving out an element - that's improvisation! Now, the students may try themselves.

Part C

I start improvising with *shuffles* and *steps*, then the student next to me joins in and also improvises with *steps* and *shuffles* in a different way. After a while, I stop, my dancing partner continues alone and then the next student joins in. This way everybody dances alone for a while, and then in pairs with overlaying rhythms. When doing this kind of exercise, I usually suggest including pauses especially when improvising in pairs or groups - this way the most exciting overlaying rhythms happen.

Part D

During the next round the participants may also use other techniques or stick with *steps* and *shuffles*.

IMPROVISATION EXERCISE 2

FLAPS + BREAK

Flaps have already been introduced and I have explained that we do 3x8 *flaps* plus one improvised *break* (over eight counts)

Part A

We stand in a circle; the music is medium tempo swing.

At first we do *flaps* and the improvised *break* all together. That means during the *break* everyone taps something different. We repeat this several times.

Part B

Each participant dances eight counts alone. Like before it's 3x8 *flaps* plus the improvised *break*. Make sure, that there is an uneven number of participants, so that everyone does the break.

Part C

Again, the students dance simultaneously - they may do *flaps*, improvised parts and *breaks* whenever they want. Every part should go over eight counts, apart from that the structure is free.

IMPROVISATION EXERCISE 3

WALKING - IMPROVISING

Choose a piece of music with a clear rhythm. We crisscross the room - doing flats on the fourth notes over two bars. Then we pause over two bars. Meanwhile we listen to the music intensively and let the rhythm work. Then we improvise over two bars and afterwards start again: walking, pausing, improvising...

Variation

The participants are free to decide if and how long they walk, improvise or pause. The pauses should be used to get inspired by the other dancers' improvisation and hence use elements for their own improvisational parts.

 # Choreography

GENERAL CONSIDERATIONS ON CHOREOGRAPHY

The core of my lessons is always a choreography. That means, I teach new techniques and combinations on the basis of choreographies and routines. There are several traditional tap dance pieces in my repertoire; those are flexibly suitable for different pieces of music. Most of my own choreographies are created for a particular piece of music.

When I started teaching, I knew exactly three traditional choreographies and I was not sure how to invent combinations or even whole choreographies.

At that time, I was also forced to listen to music intensively and extensively in order to check, if it was possible to tap-dance to it. Music started to talk to me. Sometimes students ask me, why I built a particular combination into a particular piece of music. "That's what the music asked me to do", I have to answer.

The first step to a choreography mostly is an inspiring musical piece or one, that my students wish to dance to. If possible, I gladly fulfil wishes concerning music, but I have to like it and generally speaking, it must qualify - if only in my personal opinion - for tap-dancing. Almost always a choreography develops from improvisation. Or it derives from rhythmical structures, that "demand" a specific step combination.

The first dance that I teach in adult groups, is almost always the Shim Sham Shimmy - it's **the** traditional tap dance that the majority of tap dancers all over the world learns once in their life. Leonard Reed and Willie Bryant made up this piece one hundred years ago, and nowadays there are countless variations of the original Shim Sham.

Here I will write down the version, that I teach to my students.

Furthermore I want to provide you with a choreography for beginner - intermediate level, that I originally created to Alanis Morissette's cover of Cole Porter's "Let's do it, let's fall in love" . But it is suitable for most swing standards as well.

Shim Sham Shimmy (Leonard Reed & Willie Bryant)

In my version, the rhythmical basis is binary, except for the third step, that is done on a triplet basis. There are other versions of the Shim Sham, that are completely built in swing rhythm - you can try out, what you like best.

Suggestions for music titles:
When somebody thinks you're wonderful by Brian Ferry
Honey Pie by The Beatles

1. Step - Shim Sham

8	shuf-	r
+1	fle step	r r
2	shuf-	l
+3	fle step	l l
4	shuf-	r
+5	fle step	r r
+6	step shuf-	l r
+7	fle step	r r

Repeat on the left side, then again on the right side; the last **step** becomes a **tap**!

Shim Sham Break:

8	flat	r
1	toe	l
2	step	l
3	hop	l
+(4)	step	r
+5	hop step	r l
6	step	r
7	step	l

The next step, the Cross-Over starts with rotating the lower body, that is hips, legs, knees and feet. With the first *flat* we rotate to the right, with the following *step* to the left diagonal. After two times, we perform the cross-over movement.

2. Step - Cross Over

8	flat	r
1	step	l
2	flat	r
3	step	l
4	flat	r
5	heel step	r l (cross at the front)
+6	heel	l
7	flat	r

Reverse and repeat!

Break:

8	flat	l
1	heel	l
+(2)	step	r (cross at the front)
+3	heel flat	r l
4	flat	r
5	heel	r
+(6)	step	l (cross at the front)
+7	heel flat	r r

3. Step - Tack Annie

e8	stamp stomp	l r
e1	brush tap	r r (cross at the back)
2	flat	r
e3	brush tap	l l (cross at the back)
4	flat	l
e5	brush tap	r r (cross at the back)
6	flat	r
e7	brush tap	l l (cross at the back)

This step will be performed three times, finally the last *tap* will be replaced by a *step*, so that the weight is on the left foot!

Break:

= Shim Sham Break

4. Half Break

8	flat	r
1	step	l
+3	shuffle	r
+3	step step	r l
4	flat	r
5	step	l
+6	shuffle	r
+7	step step	r l

Break:

= Shim Sham Break

For a close, I like this variation of the Shim Sham Break:

8	flat	r
1	toe	l
2	step	l
3	hop	l
+(4)	step	r
+5	hop step	r l
6	jump	r+l (outwards)
7	jump	r+l (inwards)
8	flat	r (into a pose)

The Shim Sham is a wonderful dance for beginners, because it starts simple; the third step is a bit tricky and has to be practised well. When the Shim Sham is performed, it looks good, although it is relatively simple and short.

Furthermore, you can get exciting variations out of this dance.
A popular variation is to omit the breaks, that is, you rest during the break - that works best doing a pose/freeze.

The Shim Sham also works well as a round; I like to let one group start with the first step the other group with the third step. A more advanced and rhythmically very challenging possibility is to let one group start on count 8, the other on count 1.

Try out these or other variations and let me know, what you like best!
Anyway, it's most impressive to do the round a cappella, so that the subtle overlays can be heard best.

Let's do it

MUSIC: LET'S DO IT, LET'S FALL IN LOVE (ALANIS MORISSETTE)

The dance is built in a classical 4x8 counts structure (=eight four-quarter bars).

Basic rhythm: ternary, that is swing-rhythm

We start in the song after the intro - the singing starts really slowly; when she sings "...in Spain the..." the basic tempo starts and we too.

1. Step (Intro)

1	step	r (r crosses over l)
e2	heel step	r l
e3	heel step	l r
e4	heel step	r l (l crosses over r)
e5	heel step	l r (r crosses over l)
e6	heel step	r l
e7	heel tap	l r
(8)		

1	step	r (r crosses over l)
e2	heel step	r l
e3	heel step	l r
e4	heel step	r l (l crosses over r)
e5	heel step	l r (r crosses over l)
e6	heel step	r l
e7	heel tap	l r
e(8)	step	r

Reverse everything!

2. Step

e1	brush (back) step	r r
2	heel	r
e3	brush (back) step	l l
4	heel	l
e5	shuffle	r
e6	ball change	r l
7	step	r
8	heel	r

Now you repeat this part on the left side; do a **brush (forward)** instead of **brush (back)**. Then repeat the first part.

Break:

e1	shuffle	l
e2	ball change	l r
3	step	l (to the left side)
4	heel	l
e5	shuffle	r
e6	ball change	r l
7	flat	r
(8)		

3.Step:

1	scuff	l (1/3 turn to the right)
e2	heel dig	r l
e3	ball ri-	l r
+e4	ff heel dig	r l r
e5	ball toe	r l
e6	heel step	r l
e7	brush step (back)	r r
e(8)	flat	l

Reverse on the right side, repeat on the left; each time do a 1/3 turn to the right; for the break we stand facing forward again.

Break:

1	scuff	r
2	heel	l
e3	brush step	r r (crossing over l)
e4	heel heel	r l (turn to the left)
e5	ball ball	r l
e(6)	flat	r (front)
e7	brush tap	l l
(8)		

4. Step

1	scuff	l (diagonally to the left)
e2	heel dig	r l
e3	ball shuf-	l r (crossing over l)
e4	fle step	r r
e5	heel toe	r l
e6	heel flat	r l (turn to the front)
e7	shuffle	r
+e8	step heel flat	r r l

Reverse on the right side, repeat on the left!

Break:

e1	shuffle	r
+e2	step heel flat	r r l
e3	shuffle	r
+e4	step heel flat	r r l
5	leap	r (to the right side)
e(6)	step	l (crossing backwards)
e7	leap step	r (to the right side) l (crossing forward)
8	flat	r

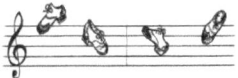 **Creativity**

There are various possibilities to support the participants in creating their own ideas. On the one hand, you can encourage them to expand their ability to improvise. (see: Improvisation-Exercises)

On the other hand, you can support them in making up their own step combinations. My experience has shown, that only some groups and participants are motivated to realize their own ideas. However, the children's groups mostly have a lot of fun with it.

As with the improvisation-exercises, it might be helpful, to offer a structure.

Here I will describe two exercises, that I use in class from time to time.

CREATIVITY EXERCISE 1

Initially we sing a short, simple song, for example *Lollypop* or *Brother John* or any song, you manage to sing well. When everybody is able to sing the song, we clap the rhythm of the melody - namely every syllable! Then the participants form groups of two or three and are supposed to make up a step combination following the rhythm of the melody.

After an agreed period we come together and each group shows their piece and the audience sings along.

CREATIVITY EXERCISE 2

I agree with the participants on four techniques, for example *steps, shuffles, toes* and *heels*.

If necessary, I demonstrate several possibilities of combining these techniques.

We agree on a beat; mostly this is the four-quarter time, but it can also be any other beat. We often agree on a song, to which the students want to make up a combination; in that case the beat is given.

We may also agree on a specific rhythmic figure; we could, for example, take the rhythm from the Shim Sham time step as a basis.

It's also possible to agree on a period, for instance two bars. Whether we do it that way depends on how much time we have and on our further procedure.

The task could therefore be: **Make up two bars in a four-quarter time; the rhythm is swing, the techniques should be *steps* and *shuffles* and *hops*; include at least one turn!**

Then the participants form groups of two or three and I set the time frame.

During this time, I go around, looking at results and helping where it is needed.

Then it's showtime! Each group may perform their results.

Extension:

After a group has shown its results, the audience gives a feedback.

Beforehand we set down the rules for giving feedback: First of all we always say something positive!!! Then we may suggest possible improvements.

After the show round and the feedback there may be a second part. During that part, the groups may improve their choreographies with the help of the feedback. Afterwards it's showtime again!

 **Body Percussion**

Within the dance, body percussion is an artform of itself. Here, we produce sound with our body, which, in principle is the same with tap dance. The difference is, that we don't use special shoes, but we clap, drum and knock on and with our body.

Tap dance and body-percussion may be combined wonderfully!

Here I want to present two short body-percussion routines to you. The first one is relatively easy and may as well work as a warm-up exercise; the second is a bit more challenging and actually is part of a longer body-percussion choreography.

BODY-PERCUSSION ROUTINE

Positioning: circle

Rhythm: binary

Direction: counterclockwise

1	flat	l
+2	clap flat	r
+3	clap flat	l
+4	clap flat	r
5	flat	l
+6	clap clap	
+7	flat clap	r
+8	clap flat	l

Reverse on the right side and repeat again on the left side. Then when beginning on the right side again, we turn to the front and move into lines.

Break:

1	stomp	r (sidewards)
+2	clap clap	
+3	flat clap	r (back to the center)
+4	stomp clap	l (sidewards)
+5	flat stomp	l r (center, side)
+6	clap clap	
+7	flat clap	r (center)
+8	flat flat	l r (to the front)

Then everything might start from the beginning or may be varied. Possible variation:

Group A starts from the top; group **B** dances simultaneously the following variation:

Group B:

1	flat	l
+2	clap clap	
+3	flat clap	r
+4	clap flat	l
5	flat	r
+6	clap flat	l
+7	clap flat	r
+8	clap flat	l

Reverse on the right side, repeat on the left. Then both groups do the break together again.

Experience has shown, that this part should be practiced in rows with me dancing in the front.

Another variation could be: the students make up their own choreography over six bars. Beginners might want to limit their repertoire to flats and claps.
Group A might possibly create one choreography and group B another; or groups of two work together.
It's always nice to use the original break at the end of the piece.

BODY PERCUSSION & TAP

(Excerpt from a longer choreography for intermediate/advanced students)

Rhythm: binary

Definition: *D* = with your flat hand onto your décolleté

O = with your flat hand onto your elevated thigh

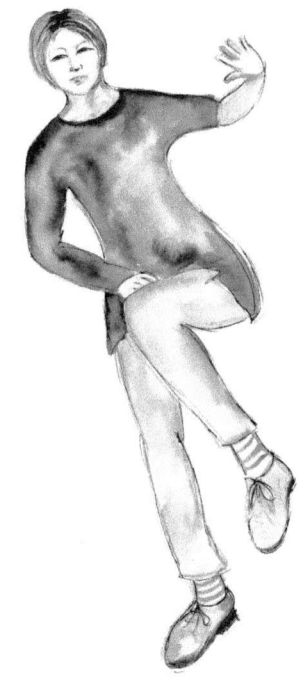

Part 1

There are two groups, facing each other. They walk towards each other and pass each other. After two bars they turn around.

1	flat	r
+2	clap flat	l
+3	clap flat	r
+4	clap flat	l
5	flat	r
+e6	clap O O	clap; then r,l, onto the left thigh
+(7)	flat	l
+8	flat flat	r l
1	flat	r
+2	clap flat	l
+3	clap flat	r
+4	clap flat	l
5	flat	r (half turn to the right)
(6)		
+7	flat clap	l
+e8	O O flat	onto the right thigh with r,l,r

Then reverse and go back to the starting position.

Transition :

With this combination, everyone walks into one or two rows, depending on the group size.

1	flat	l
2	flat	r
3	flat	l
4	flat	r
5	heel	r
e+e6	shuffle step heel	l l l
e+e7	single roll	r
e+e8	shuffle step heel	l l l

Perform this part also on the right side.

Part 2 a (2 x)

1	flat	r
+(2)	D	
+3	flat D	l
+4	D flat	r
+5	D flat	l
+(6)	D	
+7	flat D	r
+8	D flat	l

Part 2 b (2 x)

1	heel	l
e+e2	single roll	r
e3	shuffle	l
+e4	step heel flat	l l r
5	heel	r
e+e6	single roll	l
e7	shuffle	r
+e8	step heel flat	r r l

After 2a and 2b, there will be an overlay: again, we form two groups:

Overlay:

group **A**	group **B**
2 x part 2a	2 x part 2b
2 x part 2b	2 x part 2a

 **Games**

Particularly with the younger students a tap dance lesson has a lot of playful elements. Nevertheless there will always be a warm-up, exercises and choreography. On special days (before holidays, on a really hot day, or when it's somebody's birthday) or just so, we play a game or two.

During the years, I developed and picked up a repertoire of games; some of them I want to introduce to you.

GAME 1

GETTING TO KNOW EACH OTHER

This is a game for a first lesson with children, when I want to memorize their names, and we want to get to know each other.

We line up in a circle and I start: "My name is Birgit and I like to swim." I make the corresponding movement to this and then it is somebody else's turn.

Expansion:

I introduce my neighbour in the circle: "This is Alina. She likes to dance." Here again I do the corresponding movement and then it is somebody else's turn.

GAME 2

TAPPING SONGS

I especially like to play this game before Christmas; because everyone knows a lot of Christmas songs. But it surely works with other songs as well.

The students form groups of two or three and agree secretly within their group on a Christmas song. It should be a well-known song. I control that each group chose a different song and if necessary, I make suggestions.

Then each group tries to tap the melody of their song. We have practiced beforehand, how to tap a melody which is described in the chapter **Creativity**.

When every group is ready, the results are presented and the audience may guess the song. Afterwards the audience sings the song along with the respective group tap-dancing.

This game works really well for Christmas parties with parents. Before the party, we prepare and practice the Christmas song choreographies and this time the parents may guess the songs. And then we sing and tap-dance all together!

GAME 3

MEMORY IN TAP

This game works like the board game Memory, but with people.

Two children leave the room. The other children form groups of two and each group makes up a short combination; it should not be longer than two bars. The groups briefly practice to do this combination identically. Then the participants spread out in the room and the two children outside may come in .

Like in the original game, the first child (A) asks two dancers to show their combination. When they are identical, A wins two points.

Then it's B's turn. The game is over, when every group has been guessed.

GAME 4

STOP DANCE

I choose a rather dynamic music and we set the rules: when the music plays, everyone dances across the room; when the music stops, everyone freezes - nobody is allowed to move. The one who moves (first), must sit out and may possibly turn the music on and off.

This game is suitable for the end of a lesson, after we have concentrated a lot and want to dance freely a bit.

 **Music**

My first tap dance teacher was a great fan of swing music, particularly played by Big Bands. That is, why initially I thought, tap-dancing exclusively works with swing.

But actually, you can tap-dance to any musical genre!

If you like the music and if there is a definite groove and rhythm, there is no reason against tap-dancing to it.

My personal favourites are pieces, that are not so "loaded", I like to tap-dance to pieces with few instruments, that leave space for the tap rhythm.

Feel free and try out, what might work for you and your students. From time to time I ask my students to come up with their favourite songs or those they might want to tap dance to. I have discovered several new nice songs in this way.

Here are some of my favourite music pieces for class:

Ed Sheeran - *Shape of You*

Bryan Ferry - *When somebody thinks you're wonderful*

Caro Emerald - *Paris*

Cannonball Adderley - *Autumn Leaves*

Zaz - *Je veux*

Dave Brubeck - *Unsquare Dance*

Madeleine Peyroux - *Careless Love*

Harry Connick jr. - *One fine Thing*

 **Penultimate Words**

It is shortly after class. I plug my cell phone out of the system, close the windows and contemplate the past lessons. Did I see everyone of my students? I hope nobody was bored or had to struggle to much.

The door opens and a student drops in again.
"Thank you for the lesson - I enjoyed it!"

So, everything must have gone well - until next time!

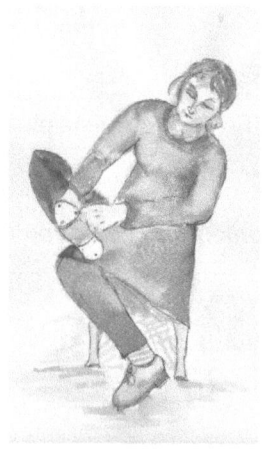

Ultimate
Words

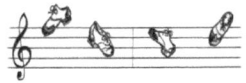

Thanks to all my students - without you, this book would not exist, because with every lesson I still learn something new.

Furthermore I want to thank all tap dancers, musicians and teachers, that inspired and supported me - in the rehearsal space, in the dance room or on stage.

I would like to mention a few by name : Irina Maué, Kurt Albert, Brenda Bufalino, Rusty Frank, Debra Bray, Josh Hilberman, Dirk David, Pia Neises, Andrea Kückmann, Bianka Sondermann and my colleagues from the Jazz Quartap!

Last but not least I want to thank Charlotte Hahn for reading and correcting my English translation!

ABOUT THE AUTHOR

Birgit Brade has been a tap dancer and a tap dance teacher for over 25 years now. Since then, she taught students of all age groups and levels, and she also realized a wide variety of stage projects. Her tap roots ly in Rhythm Tap, and her love belongs to jazz music - but not exclusively.
She does not want to commit herself to any genre - both in dance or musically and over the years she has developed her own personal style and she won't get tired to teach her skills and knowledge to her students.

Birgit Brade dances and writes and paints in Paderborn, Germany.